Goal!

The classroom door opened and
a man with a football ran in.
"Be quiet you lot!" he shouted.
"I am Mr Best. I am your
teacher today."

"Hurray!" yelled Harry.

Mr Best was the coach of the Tigers, the best football team in the world!

FINAL SCORE

Contents

Jan Burchett
and Sara Vogler

Story illustrated by
Javier Joaquin

In this story

 Harry

 Mr Best

 All Stars

 Tigers

Tricky words

- quiet
- coach
- pitch
- warming
- captain
- scored
- goalie
- match

Introduce these tricky words and help the reader when they come across them later!

Story starter

One morning, Harry heard that his teacher was ill and that a supply teacher was going to take the class. Harry was surprised when the classroom door opened and a man with a football ran in!

"All of my team have got flu,"
said Mr Best, "so you have to play
the All Stars in the Cup today."
"Hurray!" yelled the class.
They loved football.

Mr Best took the class to the football pitch. He gave them a red kit. "Now **you** are the Tigers," said Mr Best. "Start warming up!" The Tigers warmed up.

Mr Best picked the team.

Harry was the captain.

The team ran on to the pitch.

Do you think the Tigers will win?

7

Then the All Stars ran on to the pitch.

"Help!" said the Tigers. "They are very big!"

Harry kicked off. But the All Stars
got the ball. They were big and they
were fast. They scored a goal.

Harry kicked off again. The All Stars were too big and too fast.
They scored another goal.
The Tigers were two-nil down.

TIME
25:02

TIGERS
0

ALL STARS
2

"We won't win the Cup," said the Tigers.

Then Harry had an idea.

"Stop!" he yelled. "I have dropped a £20 note."

The All Stars stopped and looked for the £20.

Why did the All Stars stop?

The Tigers didn't stop.

Harry ran fast and scored a goal.

"Hurray!" yelled the Tigers.

"Two-one!"

Harry had another idea.
"Look at that spaceship!"
he yelled.

The All Stars stopped and looked.
Harry scored again.
"Hurray!" yelled the Tigers.
"Two-all!"

Harry had another idea.

"Look out!" he yelled at the goalie.

"Your lace is undone."

The goalie looked down.

Harry scored another goal.

"Hurray!" yelled the Tigers.

"Three-two!"

The match was over. The Tigers had won the Cup.

"Hurray!" yelled Mr Best and the Tigers. "Hurray for Harry!"

Quiz

Text Detective

- Why did the All Stars lose the match?
- Do you think Harry was cheating?

Word Detective

- **Phonic Focus:** Long vowel phonemes

  Page 6: Sound out the three phonemes in 'gave'. What long vowel phoneme can you hear?
- Page 8: What words do the Tigers say?
- Page 12: Can you find a word that means 'shouted'?

Super Speller

Read these words:

yelled   loved   gave

Now try to spell them!

HA! HA! HA!

Q Why can't a car play football?

A Because it's only got one boot!

Find out about

- How Lee trains at a Football Academy

Tricky words

- dreamed
- scout
- signed
- learned
- Football Academy
- tactics
- watching
- captain

Introduce these tricky words and help the reader when they come across them later!

Text starter

Do you like football? Would you like to go to a Football Academy? Read about how Lee was seen by a football scout and signed up for a big club.

Football Academy

Do you like football? Have you ever dreamed of playing for a top club? Lee loves football. He is a very good player.

When Lee was 8 years old, he played for his school. A football scout saw Lee play and saw that he was good. He signed Lee up for the Junior Team of a big club.

Lee went to the club twice a week. He trained very hard. He learned new football skills. Best of all, he played in lots of matches.

When Lee was 16 he left school.
He went to a Football Academy.
The Football Academy was run by
the football club.

Every morning at the Football Academy, Lee had lessons just like at school. Lee liked Maths and History and he worked hard at his lessons.

Every afternoon at the Football
Academy, Lee had football training.
All the players trained hard.
They all wanted to be picked to
play for the big team one day.

Footballers eat lots of meat, pasta and fruit.

The players learned how to keep fit. They learned about the right food to eat and they learned about match tactics.

The players learned about football by watching DVDs. They watched DVDs of other teams. They watched DVDs of themselves playing football.

The players learned how to behave.
They did not want to be sent off
in a match.

All the players worked very hard at the Football Academy. They all wanted to be picked to play for the big club.

One day Lee was picked to be
captain of the Youth Team.

Lee's team played well but Lee played best of all. He scored two goals!

After the match Lee had good news.
The big club signed him up. Now
Lee's dream is to play football for
his country!

Quiz

- What did Lee learn at Football Academy?
- Do you think that going to a Football Academy is a good way to get into a top club?

Word Detective

- **Phonic Focus:** Long vowel phonemes

  Page 25: Sound out the three phonemes in 'right'. What long vowel phoneme can you hear?
- Page 20: Find a word made from two smaller words.
- Page 22: How many syllables are there in 'Academy'?

Super Speller

Read these words:

played   hard   right

Now try to spell them!

HA! HA! HA!

Q Why do goalkeepers have a lot money?

A Because they are good savers!

32